Dirt

The Scoop on Soil

Written by Natalie M. Rosinsky
Illustrated by Sheree Boyd

Content Advisor: Edward Schneider, M.S., Minnesota Department of Health
Reading Advisor: Lauren A. Liang, M.A., Literacy Education, University of Minnesota, Minneapolis, Minnesota

AMAZING SCIENCE

PICTURE WINDOW BOOKS
MINNEAPOLIS, MINNESOTA

Editor: Nadia Higgins
Designer: Melissa Voda
Page production: The Design Lab
The illustrations in this book were prepared digitally.

PICTURE WINDOW BOOKS
5115 Excelsior Boulevard
Suite 232
Minneapolis, MN 55416
1-877-845-8392
www.picturewindowbooks.com

Printed in the United States of America.
1 2 3 4 5 6 08 07 06 05 04 03

Library of Congress Cataloging-in-Publication Data
Rosinsky, Natalie M. (Natalie Myra)
  Dirt : the scoop on soil / written by Natalie M. Rosinsky ; illustrated by Sheree Boyd.
    p. cm. — (Amazing science)
  Summary: Discusses the nature, uses, and importance of soil and the many forms of life that it supports.
  ISBN 1-4048-0012-3 (lib. bdg. : alk. paper)
  1. Soils—Juvenile literature. 2. Soil ecology—Juvenile literature. [1. Soils. 2. Soil ecology. 3. Ecology.] I. Boyd, Sheree, ill. II. Title.
  S591.3 .R67 2003
  577.5'7—dc21   2002005738

TABLE OF CONTENTS

What Is Dirt Made Of?. 4

It's Alive! 14

Keeping Dirt Healthy 18

Depending on Dirt 20

Experiments 22

Fast Facts: Topsoil Terrors. 23

Glossary 24

To Learn More 24

Index 24

What Is Dirt Made Of?

Dig deep. Unearth some dirt.
Hold it in your hand.

Fun fact: Dirt covers almost every place on Earth. Sometimes you can't see the dirt because it's covered by grass, buildings, roads, or water.

Dirt is a mix of different parts of nature. Crumbling rocks make up dirt. Wriggling worms and scurrying bugs live in dirt. Rotting plants and bones are part of dirt, too.

Soil is another word for dirt. Put some soil into a big glass jar and fill it with water. Stir and wait. The soil will separate into layers.

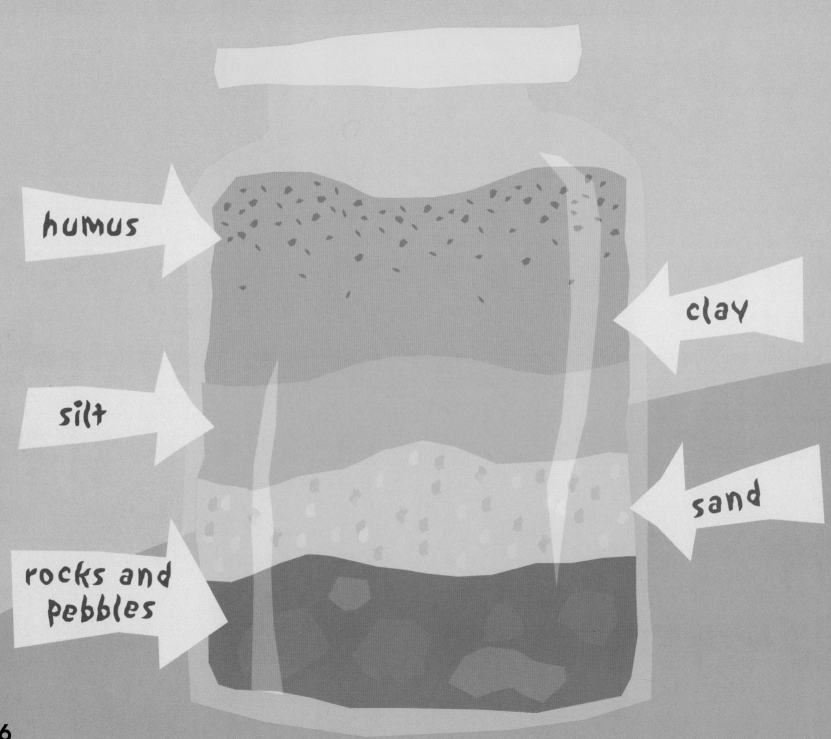

humus

clay

silt

sand

rocks and pebbles

Rocks and pebbles fall to the bottom because they're the heaviest. A lot of soil is made of rock.

Fun fact: Dirt is so interesting that soil scientists study it every day.

Sand, silt, and clay are all tiny pieces of rock that make up soil. The layer on top of the rocks and pebbles is sand.

humus
clay
silt
sand
rocks and pebbles

Use a magnifying glass to see the rainbow colors hidden in sand. Each grain has its own color—black, tan, gray, red, green, or purple.

8

Grains of sand don't fit closely together. Water runs quickly through the spaces between them. That's why sand is so dry and why sand castles crumble so fast when waves wash over them.

Silt is like sand, only silt's grains are smaller. Grains of silt fit more closely together and hold more water. Silt makes up the layer on top of the sand.

Soft, sticky clay has even smaller grains than silt. You need a microscope to see grains of clay. Clay is almost like powder. Clay is what made the water in your jar turn cloudy.

Fun fact: Clay can be red, yellow, white, tan, gray, black, or blue. People use clay to mold beautiful plates and bowls.

You might see flecks floating on top of the cloudy water. That's the dark and gooey part of soil called humus. Humus is made from rotting plants, leaves, wood, and animal matter.

Sticky humus helps hold the rocky parts of soil together. Humus is rich with food that plants need to grow green and tall.

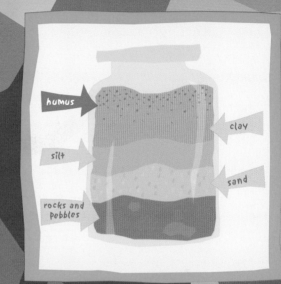

Fun fact: Soil is different in different places. Garden soil is soft and clumpy. It is a good mix of humus, sand, silt, and clay. Forest soil is often damp, full of humus from dead leaves. Soil in a muddy riverbed is soft with silt. Desert soil is sandy and dry.

13

It's Alive!

There are millions of creatures that live in soil. Beetles, sow bugs, millipedes, and worms wriggle and crawl through the dirt. Other creatures are so small that you can't see them. These soil creatures are called decomposers.

Decomposers make humus. They eat dead plants and then leave droppings. The droppings are like vitamins for the plants that grow in the soil.

Fun fact: As plants grow in soil, they use up the food in humus. Decomposers put more food back into the humus.

15

Animals can make soil better for plants in another way. Squiggling worms, trailing snails, slithering snakes, and burrowing rabbits loosen the soil as they crawl through it.

They make holes in the soil that let air and water reach the roots of thirsty plants.

Fun fact: After it rains, you can see worms wriggling along the ground. The rainwater has filled up the empty spaces in the soil. The worms have to crawl out to find air to breathe.

Keeping Dirt Healthy

Humus, water, and air are usually found in the upper layer of soil. This layer of soil is called topsoil. It is the best soil for planting.

The roots of plants hold topsoil together. Plants and trees cover topsoil so it won't get blown away by wind or carried off by rain. The loss of topsoil is called erosion. When topsoil erodes, plants have no place to grow.

Not-so-fun fact: When plants use up the food in topsoil, people can replace some of the food by adding manure or chemicals. Chemical food works for a little while, but it can kill some of the decomposers that live inside dirt. With fewer decomposers, it takes longer to make new dirt.

19

Depending on Dirt

Dirt keeps us alive. Without dirt, plants cannot grow. Without plants, animals cannot eat. Without plants and animals, people would have no food.

Dig into dirt. Pile it up and stomp it down. Let it squish between your toes. Let it sift between your fingers. As you walk along, remember all those incredible bits of nature holding you up.

21

Experiments

Ground Raid: Get permission to scoop up a handful of soil from your yard or schoolyard. Spread it out on a white paper plate. Look for leaves, sticks, seeds, bugs, worms, and rocks. Make a list of all the things you find. If you don't know the names of any small creatures you see, look up their pictures in a soil guide and find out. Draw a picture of the most interesting bug you find.

Pour some water on the area where you dug up the soil. Does the ground hold a puddle for a long time, or does the water sink in right away? What does that tell you about your soil?

What Rots First? Collect two or three kinds of fruit and vegetable scraps. For example, you might get a few potato peels, a peach pit, and a leaf of lettuce. Ask an adult to help you bury the scraps outside. Bury the scraps in the same area, but put each scrap in its own hole. Make each hole about the same size and not too deep. After you cover each hole, put a stone on top so that you'll be able to find the scraps later.

Wait a week, then go out and dig up your scraps. Which vegetable has rotted the most? Cover the scraps up again and check them in another week. Do you see worms, bugs, or other decomposers? Keep checking every week. How long does it take to see a real difference in the scraps you buried?

If you have several kinds of soil around you, try burying the same kinds of scraps in different spots. Which soil helps the scraps rot fastest?

Fast Facts: Topsoil Terrors

Creeping Deserts: Some of Earth's deserts used to be thick forests and green fields. When people cut down or burn forests on thin topsoil, the dirt is easily blown or washed away. A farmer's field also erodes if the topsoil is too thin.

As soil is lost, plants stop growing. Plants hold the water in the air close to the ground. They also provide shade and keep soil from drying out. Without plants, the land dries out and becomes a desert.

Dusty Days: During the 1930s in the United States, there was very little rain. Farmers had not been using careful farming practices and lost much of their topsoil. Dust storms developed. The storms were so bad that cattle died from breathing in the dirt. Dirt from the Midwest blew all the way to Washington, D.C.

After the dust storms, farmers planted trees along the edges of their fields. The trees broke up the steady flow of wind and slowed down erosion. Today, when you drive through the country, you can still see rows of tall trees lining the fields.

Drifting Dirt: Erosion wipes away thousands of tons of topsoil each year. Winds blow away the soil, or rain washes it into rivers and streams. Erosion can also wear away rocks. The Grand Canyon was formed by river water wearing away at hard rock for thousands of years.

Glossary

decomposers—small creatures that feed on dead plants and animals and turn them into soil

erode—to wear away

erosion—when soil is worn away by water and wind

humus—the wet, dark part of soil that is made of rotted plants and animals. Humus has food that plants need.

manure—animal droppings that people mix with soil. Manure is good for plants.

silt—soil that has grains that are smaller than sand and larger than clay. Silt is made up of tiny bits of rock.

topsoil—the layer of soil in which plants grow. Topsoil is closest to the air and sunlight and is the home of many animals and insects.

To Learn More

At the Library

Bial, Raymond. *A Handful of Dirt*. New York: Walker, 2000.

Flanagan, Alice K. *Soil*. Minneapolis: Compass Point Books, 2001.

Fredericks, Anthony D. *Under One Rock: Bugs, Slugs, and Other Ughs*. Nevada City, Calif.: Dawn Publications, 2001.

Olien, Rebecca. *Erosion*. Mankato, Minn.: Bridgestone Books, 2002.

On the Web

ThinkQuest
http://www.thinkquest.org
For science information and links

National Geographic
http://www.nationalgeographic.com
For science information

Want to learn more about dirt? Visit FACT HOUND at *http://www.facthound.com*.

Index

air, 17, 18
animals, 16–17, 20
beetles, 14
bones, 5, 12
bugs, 5, 22
clay, 8, 11, 13
decomposers, 14–15, 19, 22
desert, 13, 23
dust storm, 23
erosion, 19, 23
farmers, 23
forest, 13, 23
garden, 13
humus, 12–13, 15, 18
leaves, 12, 22
manure, 19
millipedes, 14
plants, 5, 12, 15, 17, 19, 20, 23
riverbed, 13
sand, 8–9, 13
seeds, 22
silt, 8, 10, 13
snails, 16
snakes, 16
sow bugs, 14
rabbits, 16
rain, 17, 19
rocks, 5, 7, 22
topsoil, 18–19, 23
trees, 19, 23
water, 4, 9–12, 17, 18, 22
wind, 19, 23
wood, 12
worms, 5, 14, 16, 17, 22